I Know Someone with
Epilepsy

Vic Parker

Heinemann Library
Chicago, Illinois

www.heinemannraintree.com

Visit our website to find out more information about Heinemann-Raintree books.

To order:

☎ Phone 888-454-2279

💻 Visit www.heinemannraintree.com to browse our catalog and order online.

Edited by Rebecca Rissman, Dan Nunn, and Catherine Veitch
Designed by Steve Mead and Joanna Hinton Malivoire
Picture research by Tracy Cummins
Originated by Capstone Global Library
Printed in the United States of America by Worzalla Publishing

14 13 12 11 10
10 9 8 7 6 5 4 3 2 1

Library of Congress Cataloging-in-Publication Data
Parker, Victoria.
 I know someone with epilepsy / Vic Parker.
    p. cm. — (Understanding health issues)
 Includes bibliographical references and index.
 ISBN 978-1-4329-4561-9 (hc)
 ISBN 978-1-4329-4577-0 (pb)
 1. Epilepsy—Juvenile literature. I. Title.
 RC372.2.P35 2011
 616.8'53—dc22   2010026575

Acknowledgments
We would like to thank the following for permission to reproduce photographs: AP Photo p. **23** (Mike Lawrence/The Gleaner); Corbis pp. **10** (© Ariel Skelley/Blend Images), **12** (© Bloomimage), **13** (© Tim Pannell), **14** (© Randy Faris), **27** (© Corbis); Getty Images pp. **6** (artpartner-images), **8** (Altrendo Images), **17** (Sean Justice), **19** (Robert E Daemmrich), **22** (LM Productions), **24** (Andrew H. Walker), **25** (Mick Hutson/Redferns); istockphoto pp. **4** (© Steve Cole), **5** (© Pamela Moore), **11** (© Mark Kostich), **15** (© Francisco Romero), **18** (© Bonnie Jacobs); Photo Researchers, Inc. p. **16** (Annabella Bluesky); Shutterstock pp. **20** (© Mandy Godbehear), **21** (© Andreas Gradin).

Cover photograph of a father and two children in the snow reproduced with permission of Getty Images (Caroline Woodham).

We would like to thank Ashley Wolinski and Matthew Siegel for their invaluable help in the preparation of this book.

Every effort has been made to contact copyright holders of any material reproduced in this book. Any omissions will be rectified in subsequent printings if notice is given to the publisher.

All the Internet addresses (URLs) given in this book were valid at the time of going to press. However, due to the dynamic nature of the Internet, some addresses may have changed, or sites may have changed or ceased to exist since publication. While the author and publisher regret any inconvenience this may cause readers, no responsibility for any such changes can be accepted by either the author or the publisher.

Contents

Do You Know Someone with Epilepsy? 4

What Is a Seizure? 6

How Do Seizures Affect People? 8

The Causes of Seizures 10

Who Gets Epilepsy? 12

Treatments for Epilepsy 14

Living with Epilepsy 16

At School 18

At Play 20

Living Independently 22

Famous People 24

Being a Good Friend. 26

Epilepsy: Facts and Fiction 28

Glossary 30

Find Out More 31

Index 32

Some words are printed in bold, **like this**. You can find out what they mean in the glossary.

Do You Know Someone with Epilepsy?

You may have a friend with epilepsy. Epilepsy is an illness that causes **seizures**. A seizure is something that happens in someone's **brain**. It can affect the person's senses, behavior, feelings, or thoughts for a while.

If you have a friend who has epilepsy, you can play any games you want together.

Someone with epilepsy may wear a bracelet or necklace to let others know.

Often you cannot tell that somebody has epilepsy. Unless a person is actually having a seizure, there is normally nothing unusual to see.

What Is a Seizure?

Just as computers use electricity to work, so do our **brains**. Our brains send electrical messages all around our bodies. These control everything we think, do, and say.

brain

Nerves are like long, fine threads. They carry electrical messages from our brain to all our body parts.

When a **seizure** happens, there is too much electricity in a person's brain. This can have all sorts of effects on the body, depending on the part of the brain it happens in.

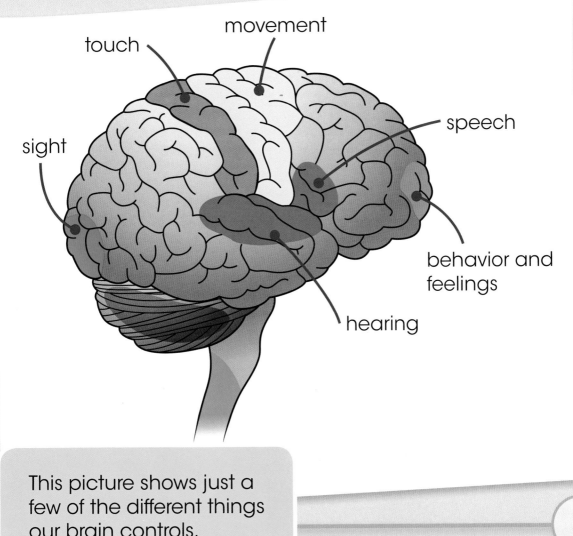

touch

movement

sight

speech

behavior and feelings

hearing

This picture shows just a few of the different things our brain controls.

How Do Seizures Affect People?

There are many different types of **seizure**. Some types of seizure make people confused. Some types make people move or make noises. Some types make people still or silent.

Some seizures can last only a few seconds. Others can last for two minutes or more.

Some people have seizures in which they fall down and their body shakes. If this happens, you can help by:

- sending someone to tell an adult and call an ambulance
- laying the person down on his or her back or side
- putting something soft under the person's head
- loosening any tight clothing
- moving everything away from the person, so he or she cannot hit things and get hurt.

The Causes of Seizures

There are many reasons why people might have **seizures**. They may have injured their head in an accident. Or they could have an illness that can affect the **brain**, like cancer.

Babies or toddlers who are sick can have a seizure if they have a very high temperature.

Doctors can do a special test to find out if a person has epilepsy.

However, some people have seizures for no reason, and these seizures happen often. This illness is called epilepsy.

Who Gets Epilepsy?

You may be slightly more likely to develop epilepsy if someone else in your family has it.

Epilepsy can happen to any person at any age. It does not matter what race they are or where they live. However, it most often begins in young children or older adults.

Doctors do not know why certain people get epilepsy, but they do know that people do not always have it for their whole lives. Young children who have epilepsy often grow out of it.

Many scientists are working hard to find out what causes epilepsy and how to prevent it.

Treatments for Epilepsy

Some people with epilepsy can have an **operation** on their **brain** to stop the **seizures**. This cure only works for a few people. Most can only try to stop seizures from happening by taking medicine.

Some people with epilepsy need more medicine than others.

Avoiding **starchy foods**, such as pasta, and eating **fatty foods** can help some people with epilepsy.

For some people the medicine works, but it can make them grumpy or unable to concentrate or keep still. A few find it does not work at all. Following a special diet can help instead.

Living with Epilepsy

Some people know when they are going to have a **seizure**. They may see, smell, or taste funny things, or they may get butterflies in their stomach.

After having a seizure, someone may feel achy, confused, and very tired.

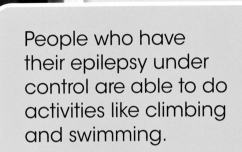

People who have their epilepsy under control are able to do activities like climbing and swimming.

People with epilepsy can do most things other people can. However, some people choose not to do activities that could be dangerous if they suddenly had a seizure.

At School

Most children with epilepsy are able to go to school with all their friends. However, many find having **seizures** embarrassing. It helps if everyone in the class knows what is happening.

A child with epilepsy may have school friends with other **medical conditions**, such as **allergies** or asthma.

Children who often have seizures—especially the kind in which they become still for a time—may miss parts of their classes. Teachers, parents, and friends should help them to catch up.

Working together can help a child with epilepsy do well at school and be happy.

At Play

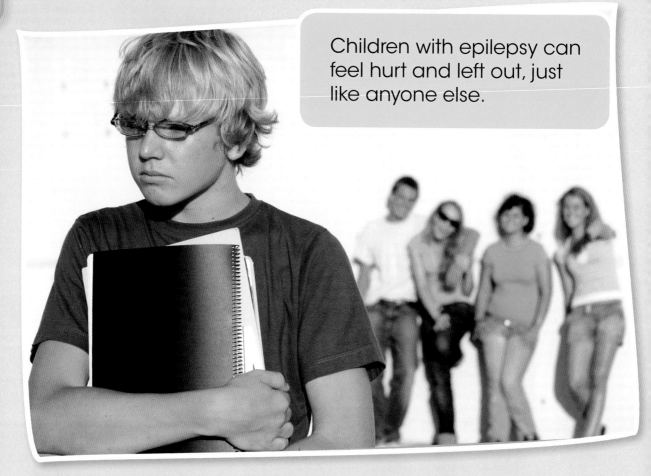

Children with epilepsy can feel hurt and left out, just like anyone else.

Most children with epilepsy love playtime and sports, just like other children. There is no reason for them not to join in fun activities.

It is important for all children, including children who have epilepsy, to have good friends and to spend time playing together. Friends can make them feel less anxious about their **seizures**. Friends can help them feel more confident.

Children with epilepsy can be very good at sports.

Living Independently

Adults with epilepsy can make choices that help them live on their own. For instance, carpet is better than hard flooring. If they fall when they have a **seizure**, they are less likely to get hurt.

Taking a shower is better than a bath, as someone having a seizure could slip under bathwater.

Some people with epilepsy use dogs or wear helmets to help protect themselves.

Some adults with epilepsy have a dog that is trained to warn them that they are going to have a seizure. They can then get to a safe place and get help.

Famous People

Danny Glover had epilepsy from ages 15 to 35. This did not stop him from becoming a top Hollywood actor who has starred in movies including *Top Gun, Antz, The Shaggy Dog,* and the *Lethal Weapon* movies.

Danny Glover used to hear a strange noise as a warning that he was going to have a seizure.

Comedian Rik Mayall takes medicines to stop him from getting seizures.

Rik Mayall is a British comedy actor who stars in many popular television shows. He has had **seizures** since he injured his head in a serious all-terrain-vehicle accident.

Being a Good Friend

There are many ways you can be a good friend to someone with epilepsy, such as:

- Include your friend in everything you do with your other friends.
- If you go swimming, stick by your friend at all times in case he or she has a **seizure**.
- If your friend has a seizure, stay calm.

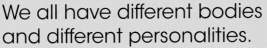
We all have different bodies and different personalities.

Living with epilepsy can be difficult at times. But there are many other ways in which we are all different. A good friend likes us just as we are.

Epilepsy: Facts and Fiction

Facts

- Ten out of every 100 Americans have a **seizure** at some point in their lives.

- People with epilepsy may be more likely to have a seizure if they are sick, stressed, tired, or hungry.

Fiction

(?) People with epilepsy are not as intelligent as other people.

WRONG! People with epilepsy can be as intelligent as anyone else.

(?) People with epilepsy cannot play video games.

WRONG! Anyone can be **sensitive** to flickering lights. But only a tiny number of people with epilepsy are affected by flickering lights. So, most people with epilepsy can play video games.

Glossary

allergy bad reaction in the body to something that a person touches, breathes, eats, or drinks

brain body part inside your skull that controls all other parts of your body and that helps you to think

fatty foods foods such as butter, milk, some fish, and cheese

medical condition health problem that a person has for a long time or for life

nerves long, thin threads that carry information between body parts and the brain

operation type of medical treatment carried out in a hospital by a doctor called a surgeon

seizure disturbance in someone's brain that can affect the senses, behavior, feelings, or thoughts for a while

sensitive quickly and easily affected by anything

starchy foods foods such as bread, pasta, and potatoes

Find Out More

Books to read

Fetty, Margaret. *Seizure-Alert Dogs* (*Dog Heroes*). New York: Bearport, 2010.

Levene, Anna. *My Friend Has Epilepsy.* West Chester, Pa.: Chrysalis, 2003.

Westcott, Patsy. *I Have Epilepsy* (*Taking Care of Myself*). New York: Gareth Stevens, 2011.

Websites

http://kidshealth.org/kid/health_problems/ brain/epilepsy.html
Visit Kids' Health to learn more about epilepsy.

http://kidshealth.org/kid/word/s/word_ seizure.html
Kids' Health explains about seizures.

www.epilepsy.com/kids/kids
This website answers common questions kids have about epilepsy.

Index

activities 17, 20
adults 22, 23
ambulance 9

bath 22
body 6, 7, 9
brain 4, 6, 7, 10, 14

children 12, 13, 18, 20, 21
clothing 9

doctors 11, 13
dogs 23

flooring 22
food 15
friends 4, 18, 19, 21, 26, 27

head 9, 10, 25
helmets 23

illness 4, 10, 11

medical condition 18
medicine 14, 15

nerves 6

operation 14

parents 19
play 4, 20, 21

school 18, 19
seizures 4, 5, 7, 8, 9, 10, 11, 14,
    16, 17, 18, 19, 21, 22, 23, 24,
    25, 26, 28
shower 22
sports 20, 21